The Age of Dinosaurs

Meet Stegosaurus

Written by Henley Miller

Illustrations by Leonello Calvetti and Luca Massini

Cavendish Square
New York

Published in 2014 by Cavendish Square Publishing, LLC
303 Park Avenue South, Suite 1247, New York, NY 10010

Copyright © 2014 by Cavendish Square Publishing, LLC

First Edition

No part of this publication may be reproduced, stored in a retrieval system, or transmitted in any form or by any means—electronic, mechanical, photocopying, recording, or otherwise—without the prior permission of the copyright owner. Request for permission should be addressed to Permissions, Cavendish Square Publishing, 303 Park Avenue South, Suite 1247, New York, NY 10010. Tel (877) 980-4450; fax (877) 980-4454.

Website: cavendishsq.com

This publication represents the opinions and views of the author based on his or her personal experience, knowledge, and research. The information in this book serves as a general guide only. The author and publisher have used their best efforts in preparing this book and disclaim liability rising directly or indirectly from the use and application of this book.

CPSIA Compliance Information: Batch #WW14CSQ

All websites were available and accurate when this book was sent to press.

Library of Congress Cataloging-in-Publication Data

Miller, Henley.
Meet stegosaurus / by Henley Miller.
p. cm. — (The age of dinosaurs)
Includes index.
ISBN 978-1-62712-604-5 (hardcover) ISBN 978-1-62712-605-2 (paperback) ISBN 978-1-62712-606-9 (ebook)
1. Stegosaurus — Juvenile literature. I. Miller, Henley. II. Title.
QE862.S3 D35 2014
567.913—dc23

Editorial Director: Dean Miller
Art Director: Jeffrey Talbot
Designer: Joseph Macri
Photo Researcher: Julie Alissi, J8 Media
Production Manager: Jennifer Ryder-Talbot
Production Editor: Andrew Coddington

Illustrations by Leonello Calvetti and Luca Massini.

The photographs in this book are used by permission and through the courtesy of: Ron and Patty Thomas,/Iconica/Getty Images, 8; Piriya Photography/Flickr Open/Getty Images, 8; David Henderson/OJO Images/Getty Images, 8; Thinkstock/Comstock Images/Getty Images, 8; EvaK/Stegosaurus Senckenberg/EvaK/GNU Free Documentation License, 20; Andrew Bret Wallis/The Image Bank/Getty Images, 21.

Printed in the United States of America

CONTENTS

1. A CHANGING WORLD — 4
2. A GIANT PORCUPINE — 6
3. FINDING STEGOSAURUS — 8
4. BIRTH — 10
5. FEEDING TIME — 12
6. THIRST — 14
7. DEFENSE — 16
8. INSIDE STEGOSAURUS — 18
9. FINDING STEGOSAURUS FOSSILS — 20
10. THE STEGOSAURS — 22
11. THE GREAT EXTINCTION — 24
12. A DINOSAUR'S FAMILY TREE — 26

A SHORT VOCABULARY OF DINOSAURS — 28
DINOSAUR WEBSITES — 30
MUSEUMS — 31
INDEX — 32

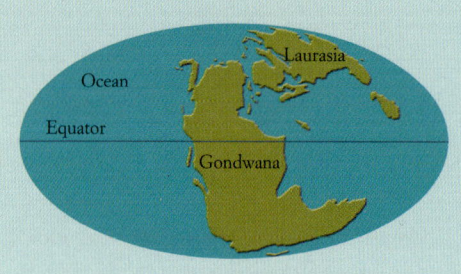

Late Triassic
227 – 206 million years ago.

Early Jurassic
206 – 176 million years ago.

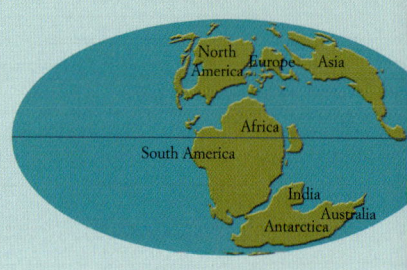

Middle Jurassic
176 – 159 million years ago.

A CHANGING WORLD

Earth's long history began 4.6 billion years ago. Dinosaurs were among the most fascinating animals from Earth's long past.

The word "dinosaur" originates from the Greek words *deinos* and *sauros*, which together mean "fearfully great lizards."

To understand dinosaurs we need to understand geological time, the life time of our planet. Earth history is divided into eras, periods, epochs, and ages. The dinosaur era, called the Mesozoic Era, is divided in three periods: Triassic, which lasted 42 million years; Jurassic, 61 million years; and Cretaceous, 79 million years. Dinosaurs ruled the world for over 160 million years.

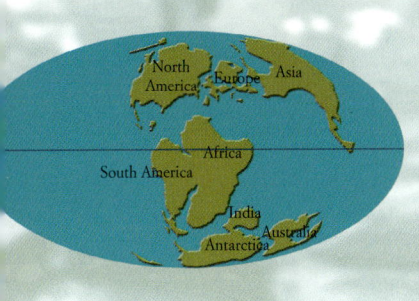

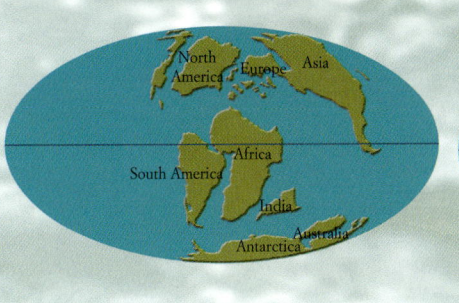

Late Jurassic
159 – 144 million years ago.

Early Cretaceous
144 – 99 million years ago.

Late Cretaceous
99 – 65 million years ago.

Man never met dinosaurs: they had disappeared nearly 65 million years before man's appearance on Earth.

The dinosaur world differed from our world. The climate was warmer, the continents were different, and grass did not even exist!

A GIANT PORCUPINE

Stegosaurus is an Ornithischian dinosaur with plates and spines on its back and tail. For this reason, they are also known by the name "spiny dinosaurs."

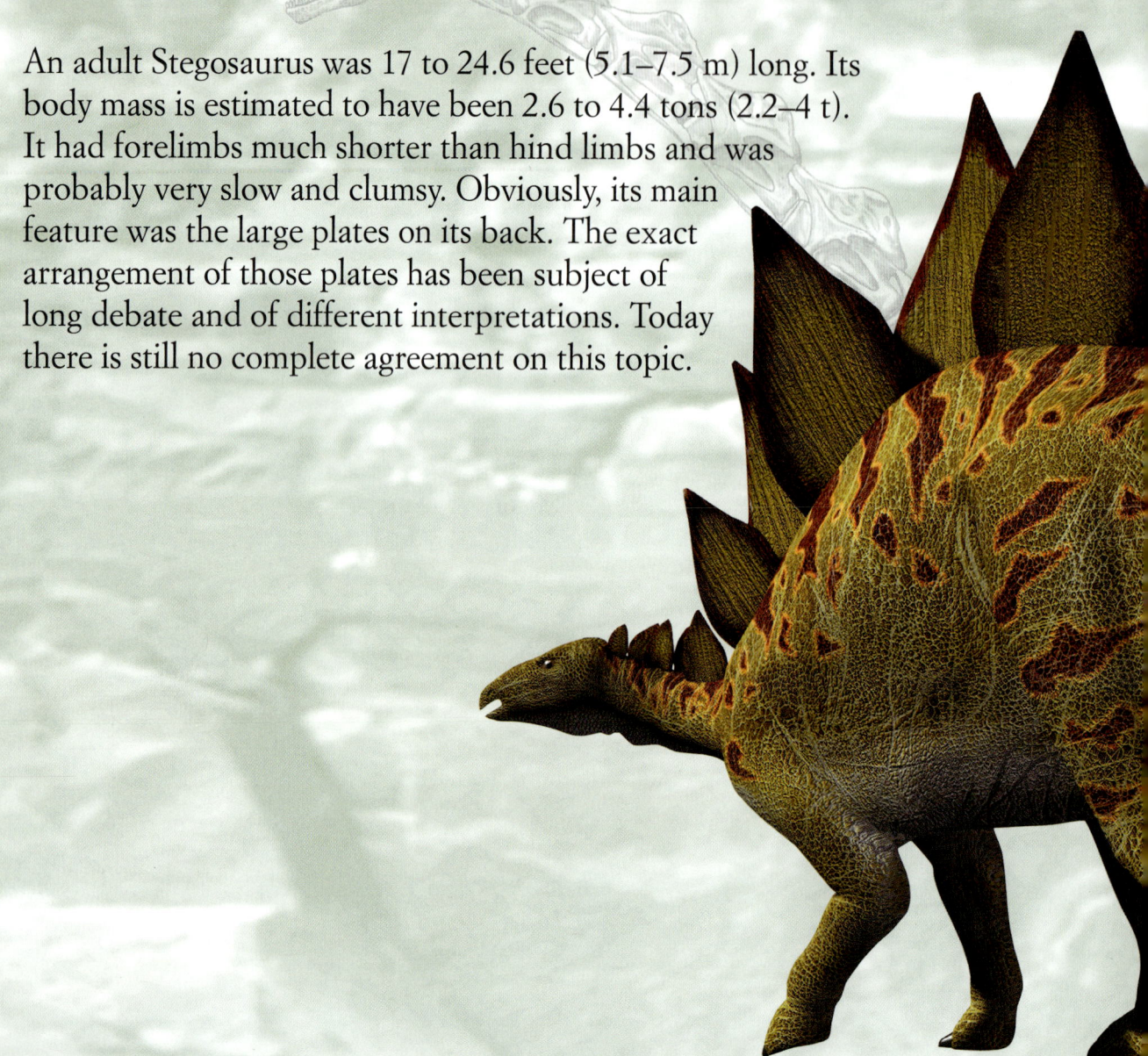

An adult Stegosaurus was 17 to 24.6 feet (5.1–7.5 m) long. Its body mass is estimated to have been 2.6 to 4.4 tons (2.2–4 t). It had forelimbs much shorter than hind limbs and was probably very slow and clumsy. Obviously, its main feature was the large plates on its back. The exact arrangement of those plates has been subject of long debate and of different interpretations. Today there is still no complete agreement on this topic.

A range of thoughts exists about what those plates did. Early on, scientists thought they were used only for defense. But now scientists hypothesize that they helped regulate the Stegosaurus' body temperature.

The stegosaur's throat and part of its neck were protected by small semi-circular bony plates, like plates of medieval armor.

7

FINDING STEGOSAURUS

Stegosaurus lived at the end of the Late Jurassic Period, 155–148 million years ago, in North America. Up to now, its remains have been collected only in Colorado, Utah, Wyoming, and New Mexico.

1. Wyoming
2. Colorado 
3. Utah 
4. New Mexico

The Western part of North America in the Late Jurassic Period. The dark brown spot indicates mountains, the lighter area represents a depression, and the red dots are findings of Stegosaurus fossils.

BIRTH

Like all the dinosaur hatchlings, Stegosaurus came into the world from eggs laid by its mother. The young did not have the large plates on their backs, but possibly only small bumps. The same is true for the spines at the end of the tail. Without protection, the eggs and the hatchlings would be victims of small-sized predator dinosaurs and agile Jurassic crocodiles.

11

FEEDING TIME

The region of the North America where Stegosaurus lived around 150 million years ago was a semi-dry plain crossed by meandering rivers. This plain was probably similar to the savannah that exists today in eastern Africa, but without the tall grass. In fact, grass appeared on Earth many millions of years after the extinction of the dinosaurs. Plants were also much different from those which dominate today. Stegosaurus fed on leaves and on the tender parts of Jurassic plants.

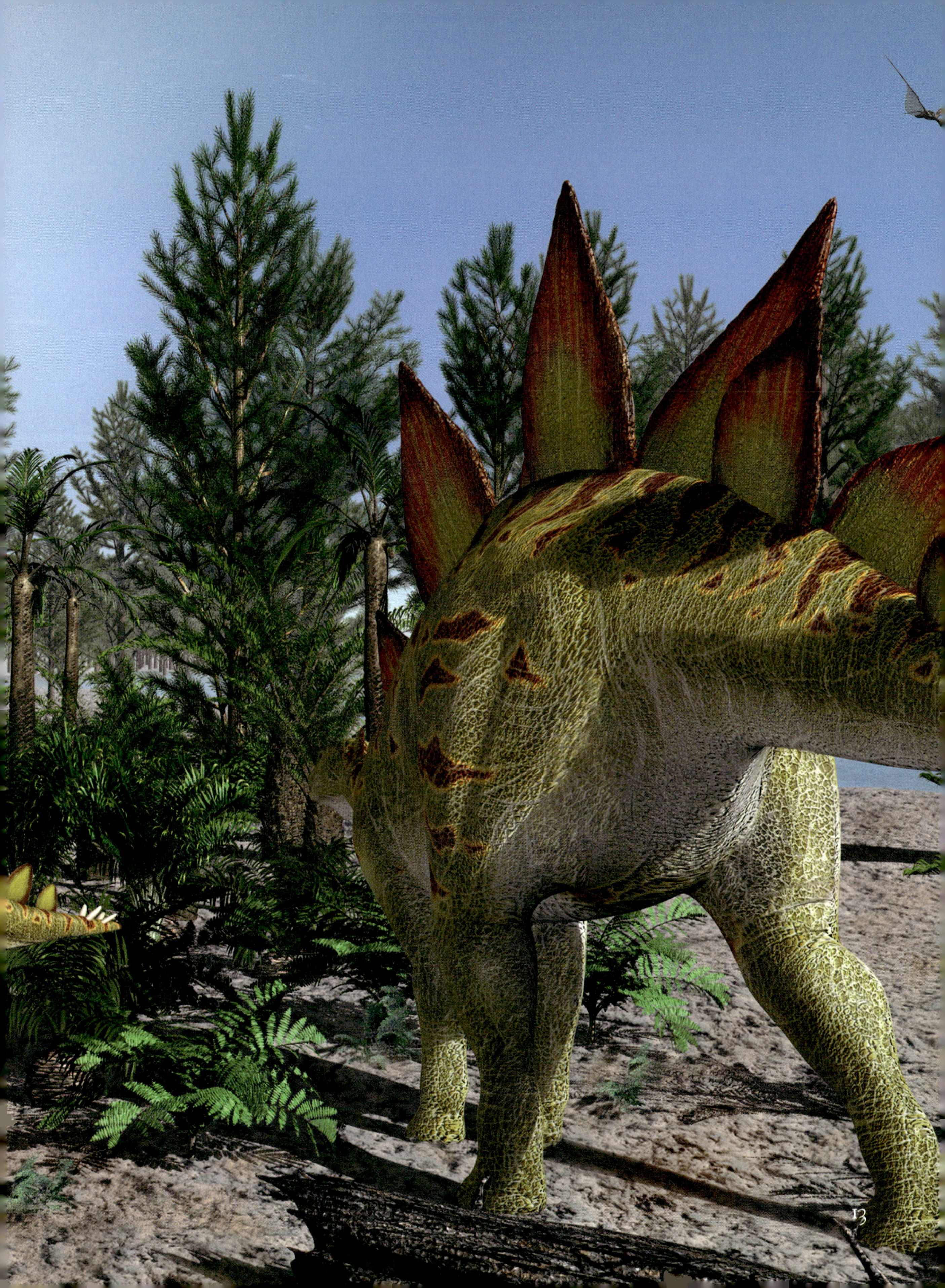

THIRST

One of the main problems that the stegosaurs had to face repeatedly in their lifetimes were periods of drought. In fact, during the dry season watering holes dried up, leaving just muddy pools. Herds of dinosaurs crowded around these pools looking for a sip of water. Many exhausted animals ended up stuck in the mud and dying of starvation.

Predators tried to take advantage of these trapped or dead animals, but sometimes ended up victims of the quicksand. Only the beginning of the rainy season guaranteed that the stegosaurs would not die of thirst.

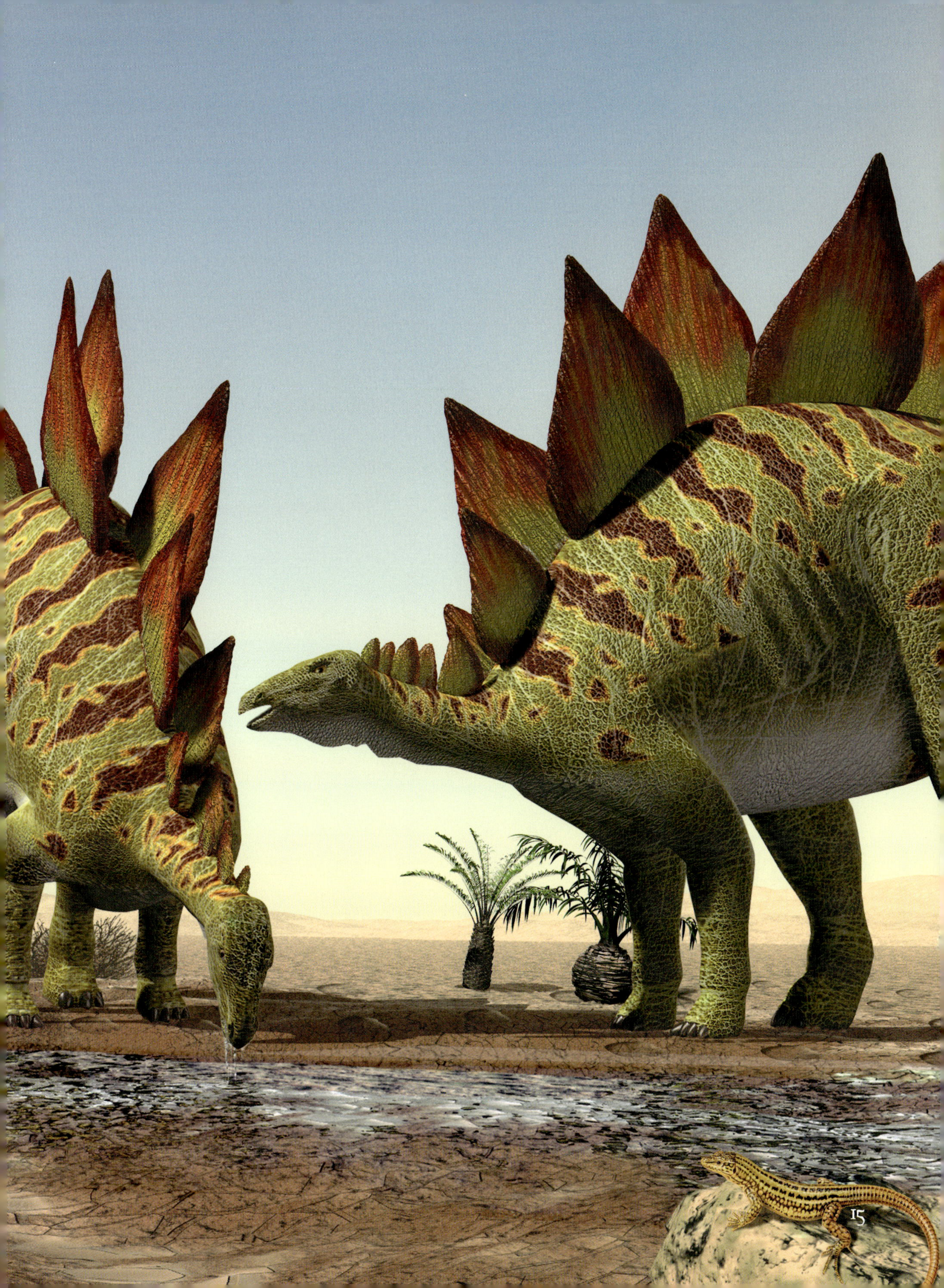

DEFENSE

Stegosaurus was a slow animal that could not outrun an attacking predator. It solved this problem by using its large size and some highly specialized body structures. In fact, the tip of the stegosaur's tail had four long spines facing upward and outward, and could be used to hit and hurt its attackers. The large plates on the back, at the base of the tail, and on the neck made it harder for predators to bite those parts of the body. Even so, it is probable that Allosaurus, the largest (up to 30 feet (9.1 m) in length) predator at the time, sometimes tried to kill and eat these spiny animals.

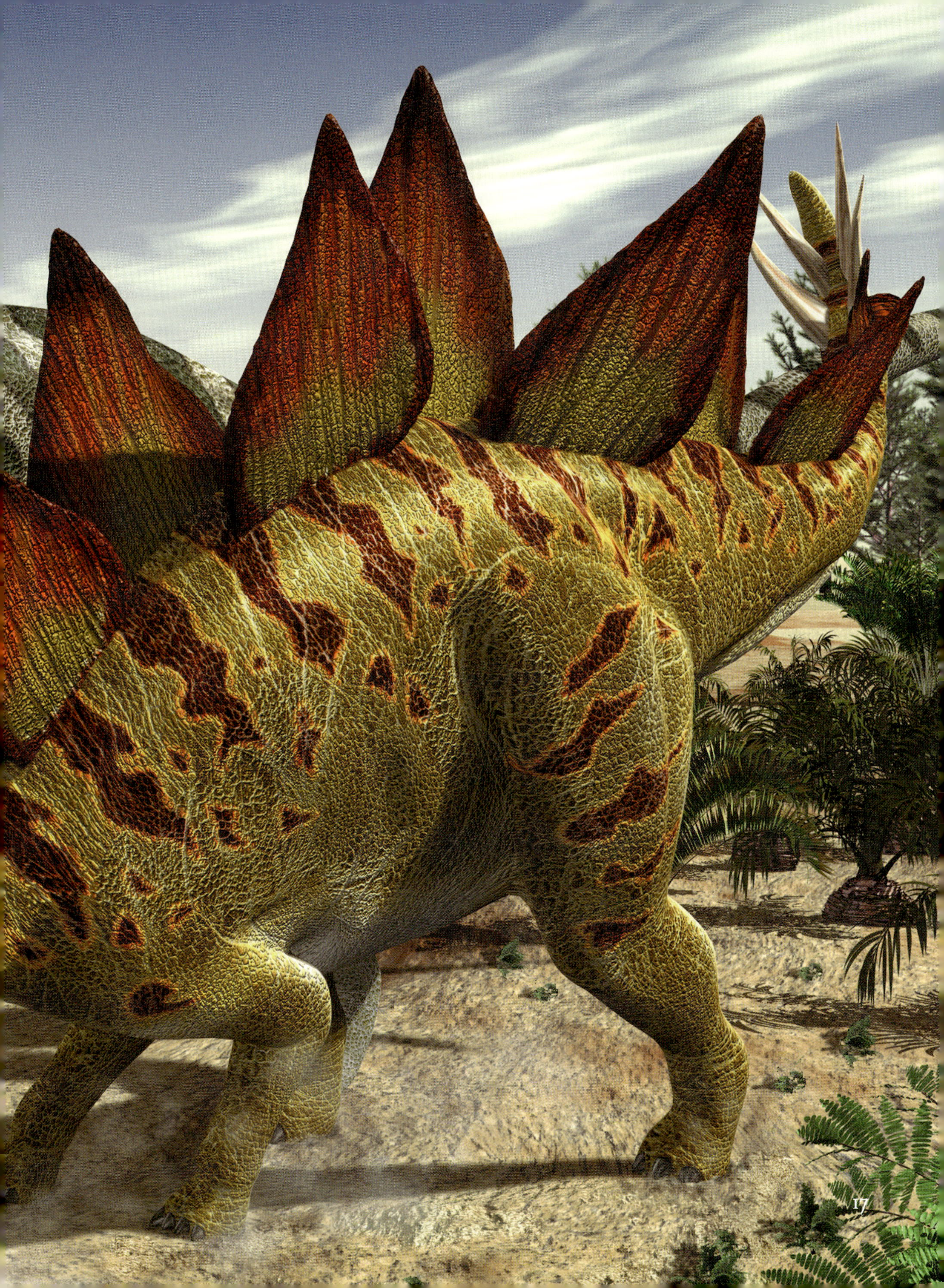

INSIDE STEGOSAURUS

The head of Stegosaurus was about a foot long at its longest point, very small compared to its body size. Its teeth were numerous and relatively small. Such teeth are easy to identify even if incomplete.

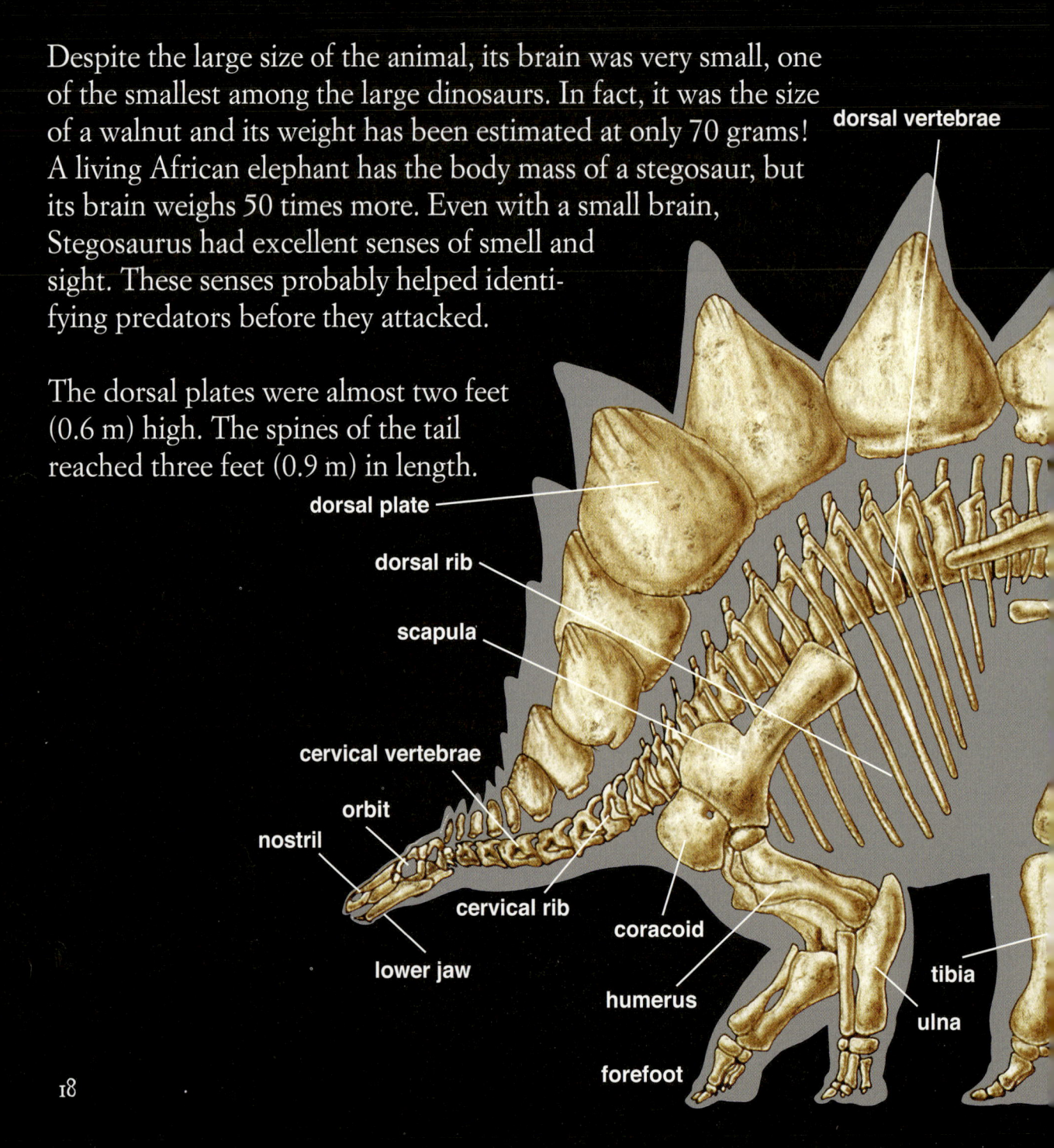

Despite the large size of the animal, its brain was very small, one of the smallest among the large dinosaurs. In fact, it was the size of a walnut and its weight has been estimated at only 70 grams! A living African elephant has the body mass of a stegosaur, but its brain weighs 50 times more. Even with a small brain, Stegosaurus had excellent senses of smell and sight. These senses probably helped identifying predators before they attacked.

The dorsal plates were almost two feet (0.6 m) high. The spines of the tail reached three feet (0.9 m) in length.

dorsal vertebrae
dorsal plate
dorsal rib
scapula
cervical vertebrae
orbit
nostril
cervical rib
coracoid
lower jaw
humerus
tibia
ulna
forefoot

Side view of the skull

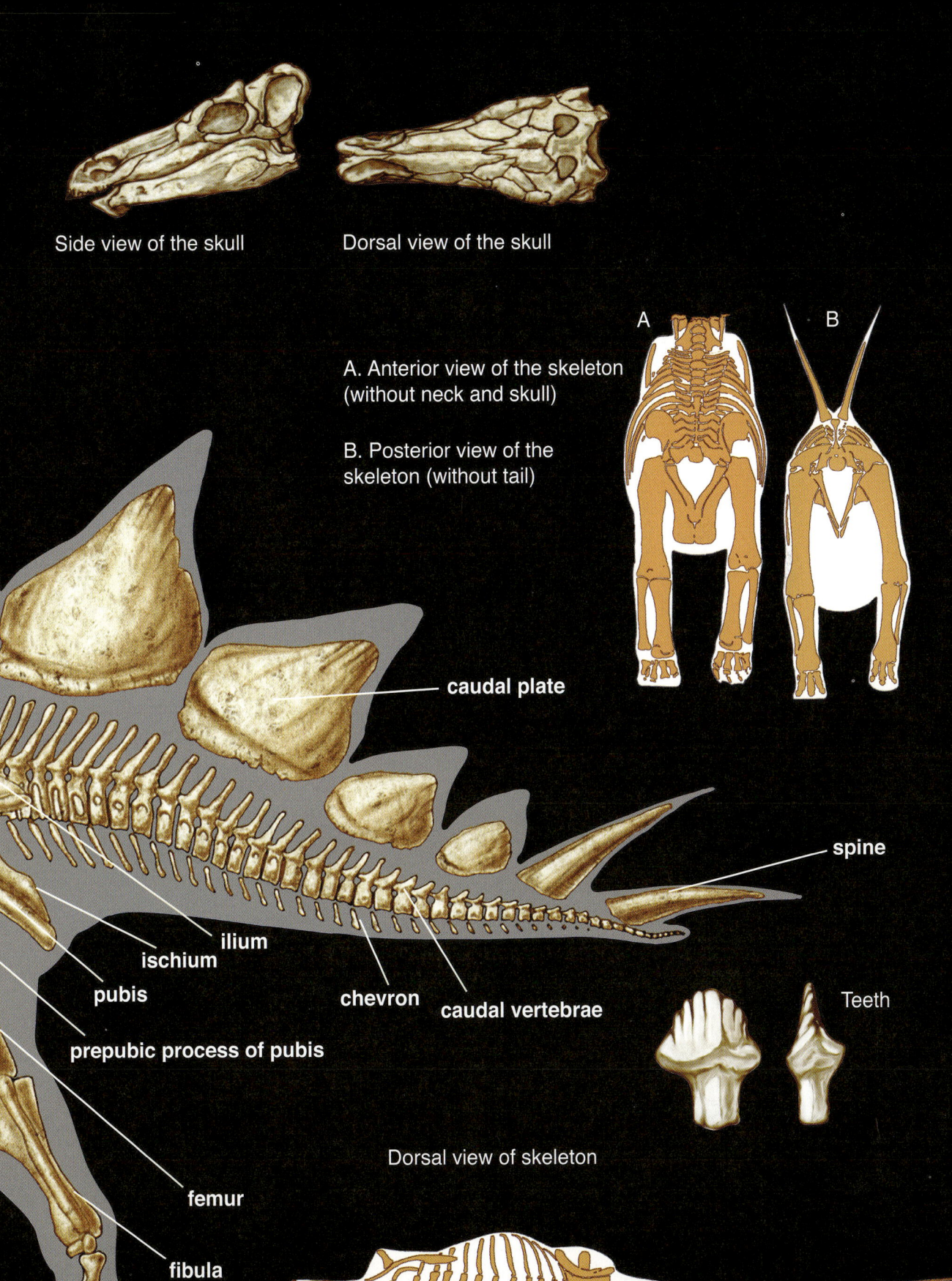

Dorsal view of the skull

A. Anterior view of the skeleton (without neck and skull)

B. Posterior view of the skeleton (without tail)

caudal plate

spine

ilium

ischium

pubis

chevron

caudal vertebrae

Teeth

prepubic process of pubis

femur

Dorsal view of skeleton

fibula

FINDING STEGOSAURUS FOSSILS

The first skeletal remains of Stegosaurus were found in Colorado in 1877, and were soon named by the paleontologist Othniel C. Marsh. The name originates from the Greek and means "roofed reptile," referring to the plates on its back. At that time they were thought to lay flat on the back, like tiles on a roof.

Up to now, at least two nearly complete skeletons with skulls, two partial skeletons and at least thirty incomplete skeletal portions of Stegosaurus have been recovered. They belong mostly to adult or nearly adult individuals, but rare remains of young have also been collected.

At the Dinosaur National Monument of Vernal, Utah, near the Colorado border, it is possible to see the bones of Stegosaurus still preserved in the rock wall along with those of large sauropods such as Diplodocus and Camarasaurus, as they were deposited 150 million years ago.

Stegosaurus was officially chosen as the state fossil of Colorado.

THE STEGOSAURS

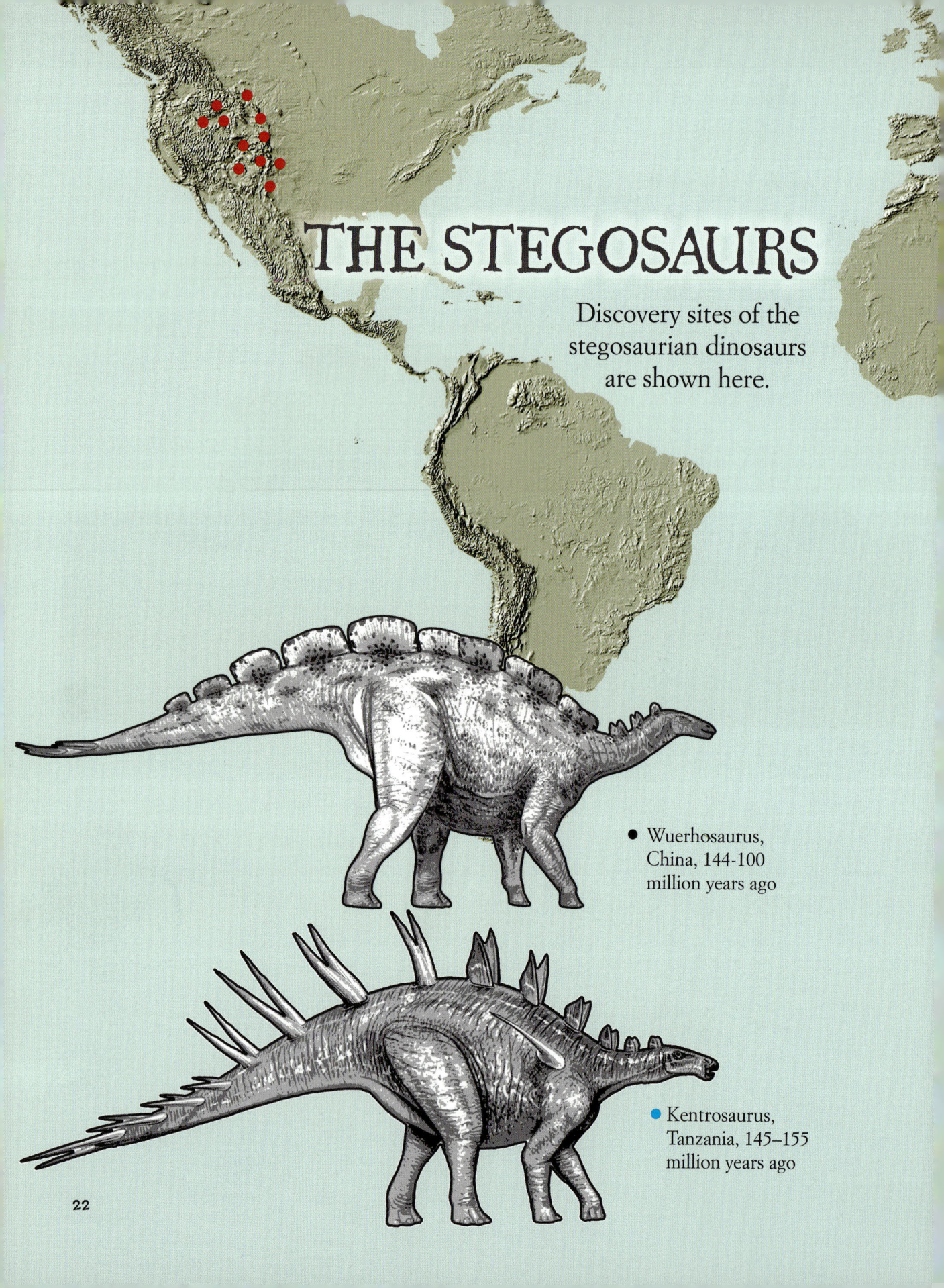

Discovery sites of the stegosaurian dinosaurs are shown here.

- Wuerhosaurus, China, 144-100 million years ago

- Kentrosaurus, Tanzania, 145–155 million years ago

- Stegosaurus, United States, 148–154 million years ago

23

THE GREAT EXTINCTION

Sixty-five million years ago (about 80 million years after the time of Stegosaurus), dinosaurs became extinct. Scientists think a large meteorite hitting the earth caused this extinction. A wide crater caused by a meteorite exactly 65 million years ago has been located along the coast of Mexico. The dust suspended in the air by the impact would have obscured the sunlight for a long time, causing a drastic drop in temperature and killing many plants.

The plant-eating dinosaurs would have frozen or starved to death. Meat-eating dinosaurs would have also died without their food supply. However, some scientists believe dinosaurs did not die out completely, and that present-day chickens and other birds are, in a way, the descendants of the large dinosaurs.

25

A DINOSAUR'S FAMILY TREE

The oldest dinosaur fossils are 220–225 million years old and have been found all over the world.

Dinosaurs are divided into two groups. Saurischians are similar to reptiles, with the pubic bone directed forward, while the Ornithischians are like birds, with the pubic bone directed backward.

Saurischians are subdivided in two main groups: Sauropodomorphs, to which quadrupeds and vegetarians belong; and Theropods, which include bipeds and predators.

Ornithischians are subdivided into three large groups: Thyreophorans which include the quadrupeds Stegosaurians and Ankylosaurians; Ornithopods; and Marginocephalians subdivided into the bipedal Pachycephalosaurians and the mainly quadrupedal Ceratopsians.

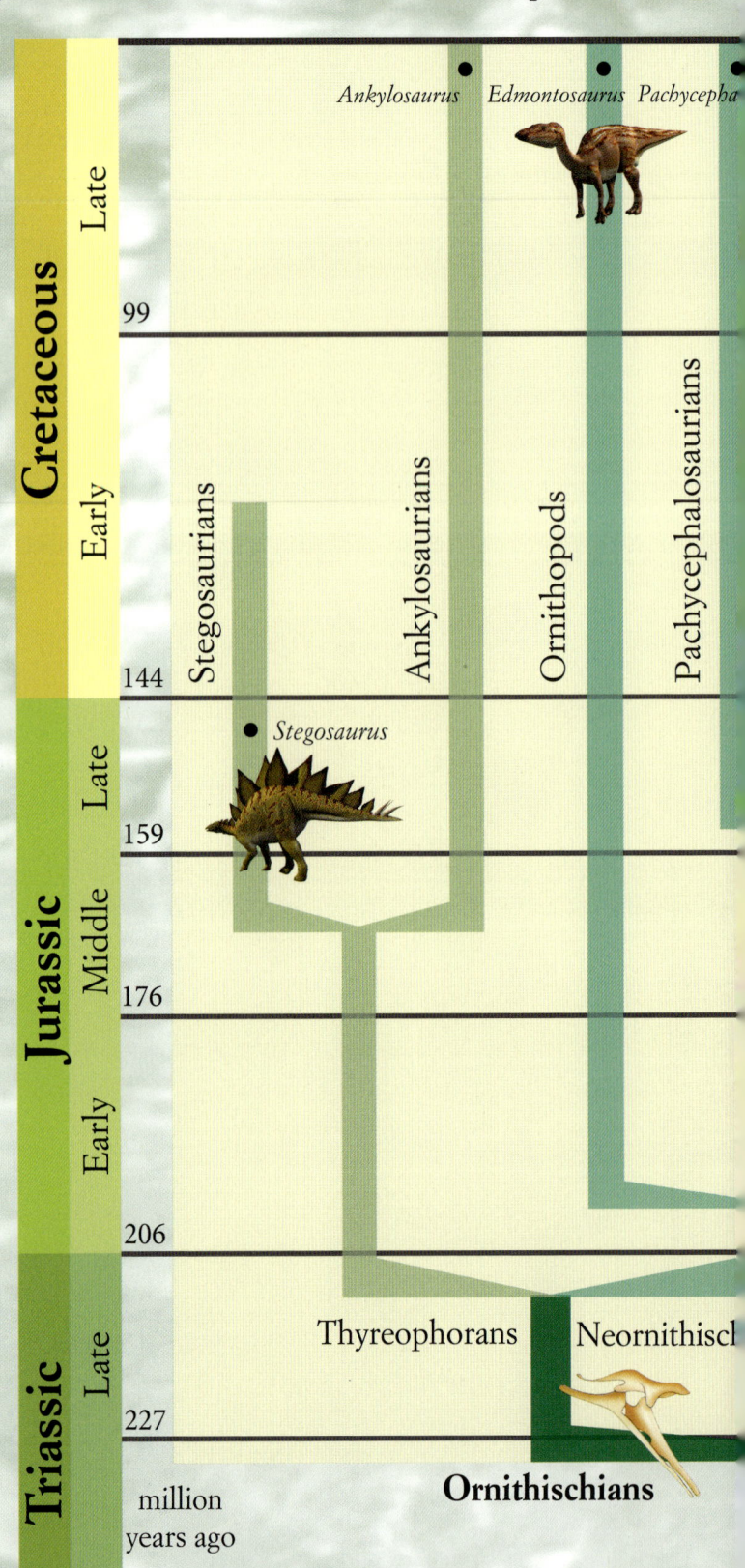

Ankylosaurus *Edmontosaurus* *Pachycepha*

Stegosaurus

Stegosaurians
Ankylosaurians
Ornithopods
Pachycephalosaurians

Period	Epoch	Mya
Cretaceous	Late	99
Cretaceous	Early	144
Jurassic	Late	159
Jurassic	Middle	176
Jurassic	Early	206
Triassic	Late	227

million years ago

Thyreophorans   Neornithisc

Ornithischians

Dinosauria

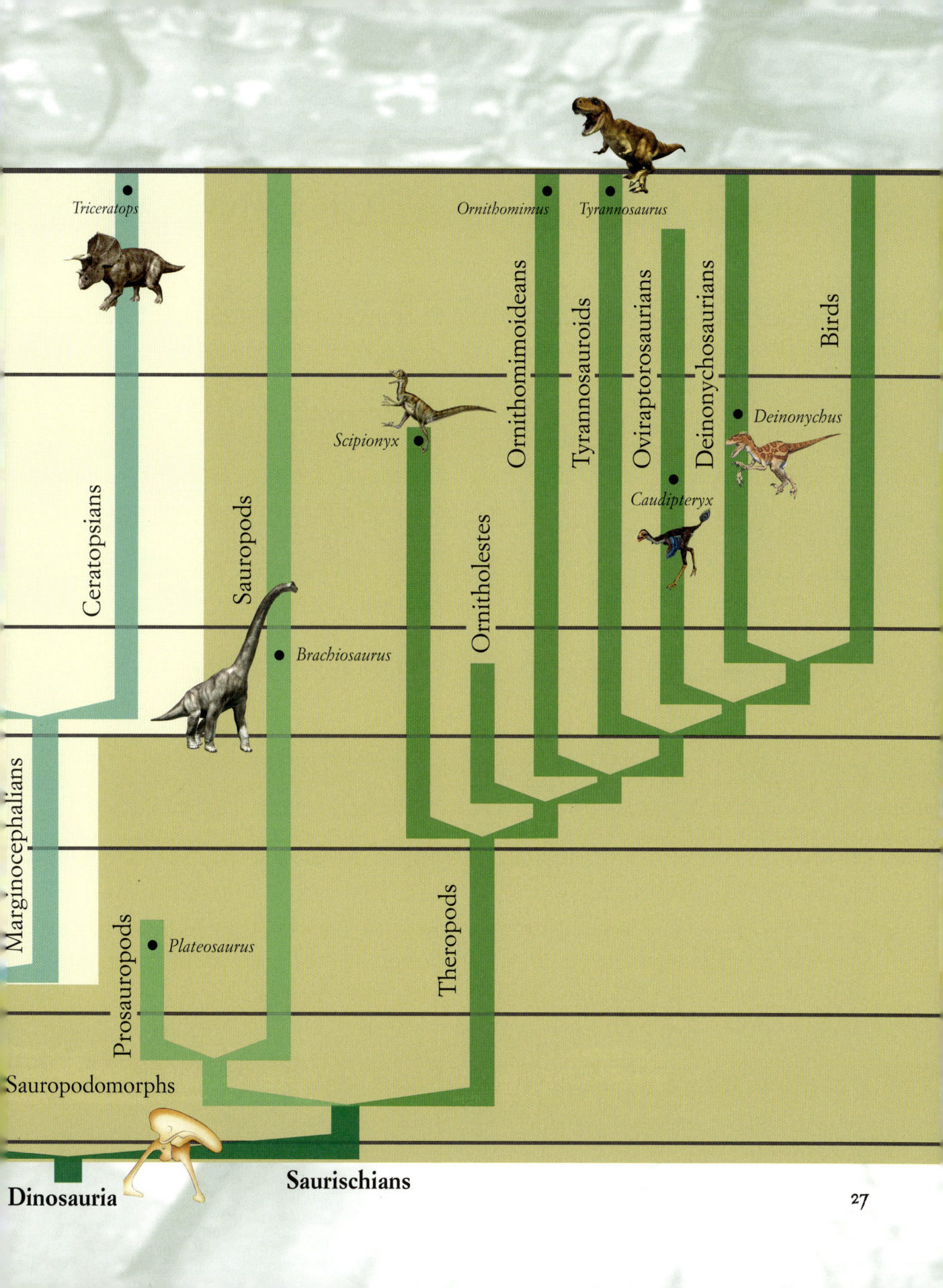

Saurischians

- Marginocephalians
  - Ceratopsians
    - *Triceratops*
- Sauropodomorphs
  - Prosauropods
    - *Plateosaurus*
  - Sauropods
    - *Brachiosaurus*
- Theropods
  - Ornitholestes
    - *Scipionyx*
  - Ornithomimoideans
    - *Ornithomimus*
  - Tyrannosauroids
    - *Tyrannosaurus*
  - Oviraptorosaurians
    - *Caudipteryx*
  - Deinonychosaurians
    - *Deinonychus*
  - Birds

A SHORT VOCABULARY OF DINOSAURS

Bipedal: pertaining to an animal moving on two feet alone, almost always those of the hind legs.

Bone: hard tissue made mainly of calcium phosphate; single element of the skeleton.

Carnivore: a meat-eating animal.

Caudal: pertaining to the tail.

Cenozoic Era (Caenozoic, Tertiary Era): the interval of geological time between 65 million years ago and present day.

Cervical: pertaining to the neck.

Claws: the fingers and toes of predator animals end with pointed and sharp nails, called claws. Those of plant-eaters end with blunt nails, called hooves.

Cretaceous Period: the interval of geological time between 144 and 65 million years ago.

Egg: a large cell enclosed in a porous shell produced by reptiles and birds to reproduce themselves.

Epoch: a division of geologic time.

Evolution: changes in the character states of organisms, species and higher ranks through time.

Feathers: outgrowth of the skin of birds and some other dinosaurs, used in flight and in providing insulation and protection of the body. They evolved from reptilian scales.

Forage: to wander in search of food.

Fossil: evidence of the life in the past. Not only bones, but footprints and trails made by animals, as well as dung, eggs, or plant resin, when fossilized, is a fossil.

Herbivore: a plant-eating animal.

Jurassic Period: the interval of geological time between 206 and 144 million years ago.

Mesozoic Era (Mesozoic, Secondary Era): the interval of the geological time between 248 and 65 million years ago.

Pack: group of predator animals acting together to capture the prey.

Paleontologist: scientists who study and reconstruct prehistoric life.

Paleozoic Era (Paleozoic, Primary Era): the interval of geological time between 570 and 248 million years ago.

Predator: an animal that preys on other animals for food.

Raptor (raptorial): a bird of prey, such as an eagle, hawk, falcon, or owl.

Rectrix (plural rectrices): any of the larger feathers in a bird's tail that are important in helping its flight direction.

Scavenger: an animal that eats dead animals.

Skeleton: a structure of animal body made of several different bones. One primary function is also to protect delicate organs such as the brain, lungs, and heart.

Skin: the external, thin layer of the animal body. Skin cannot fossilize unless it is covered by scales, feathers, or fur.

Skull: bones that protect the brain and the face.

Teeth: tough structures in the jaws used to hold, cut, and sometimes process food.

Terrestrial: living on land.

Triassic Period: the interval of geological time between 248 and 206 million years ago.

Vertebrae: the single bones of the backbone; they protect the spinal cord.

DINOSAUR WEBSITES

Dinosaur Train (pbskids.com/dinosaurtrain/): From the PBS show Dinosaur Train, you can have fun watching videos, printing out pages to color, play games, and learn lots of facts about so many dinosaurs!

The Natural History Museum (http://www.nhm.ac.uk/kids-only/dinosaurs/): Take a quiz to see how much you know about dinosaurs or a quiz to tell you what type of dinosaur you'd be! There's also a fun directory of dinosaurs, including some cool 3D views of your favorites.

Discovery Channel Dinosaur videos (http://dsc.discovery.com/video-topics/other/dinosaur-videos): Watch almost 100 videos about the life of dinosaurs!

Dinosaurs for Kids (www.kidsdinos.com): There's basic information about most dinosaur types, and you can play dinosaur games, vote for your favorite dinosaur, and learn about the study of dinosaurs, paleontology.

Dino Data (www.dinodata.org): Get the latest news on dinosaur research and discoveries. This site is pretty advanced, so you may need a teacher's or parent's help to find what you're looking for.

MUSEUMS

Yale Peabody Museum of Natural History, 170 Whitney Avenue, New Haven, CT 06520-8118

American Museum Natural History, Central Park West at 79th Street, New York, NY 10024-5192

The Field Museum, 1400 So. Lake Shore Drive, Chicago, IL 60605-2496

Carnegie Museum of Natural History, 4400 Forbes Avenue, Pittsburgh, PA 15213-4080

National Museum of Natural History, the Smithsonian Institution, 10th Street and Constitution Avenue NW, Washington, DC 20560-0136

Museum of the Rockies, 600 W. Kagy Boulevard, Bozeman, MT 59717

Denver Museum of Nature and Science, 2001 Colorado Boulevard, Denver, CO 80205

Dinosaur National Monument, Highway 40, Dinosaur, CO 81610

Sam Noble Museum of Natural History, 2401 Chautauqua, Norman, OK 73072-7029

Museum of Paleontology, University of California, 1101 Valley Life Sciences Bldg., Berkeley, CA 94720-4780

Royal Tyrrell Museum of Palaeontology, Hwy 838, Drumheller, AB T0J 0Y0, Canada

INDEX

Page numbers in **boldface** are images.

....

bipedal, 26
bone, 21, 26

caudal
    caudal plate, **19**
    caudal vertebrae, **19**
cervical
    cervical rib, **18**
    cervical vertebrae, **18**
Cretaceous Period, 4, **5**, **26–27**

egg, 10
epoch, 4

fossil, **9**, 20–21
    oldest fossil, 26
    state fossil, 21

Jurassic Period, 4, **4**, 8, **9**, **26–27**

Mesozoic Era, 4

paleontologist, 20
predator, 10, 14, 16, 18, 26

reptile, 26
    "roofed reptile," 20

skeleton, **19**, 20
skull, **19**, 20
Stegosaurus
    size, 6, 18
    speed, 6
    where discovered, 8, **9**, 20–23

teeth, 18
Triassic Period, 4, **4**, **26–27**

vertebrae, **18**, **19**